THIS GUIDE BELONGS TO

AS THEY PARENT

Date / Year

Kind Words from Parents, Grandparents, & Experts in Parenting

Sandra Stanley

Author of *Breathing Room*, and co-author of *Parenting: Getting it Right*, foster care advocate, mother of three

We all know where we want to end up in our parenting, but how to get there can seem like an unsolved mystery. The *Phase Guides* give us a resource to help out. They help to guide parents and caregivers through the different seasons of raising children, and provide a road map to parenting in such a way that we finish up with very few regrets.

Sissy Goff M.Ed., LPC-MHSP

Co-director of Child and Adolescent Counseling at Daystar Counseling Ministries, speaker and author of 12 books, including *Brave*

It's hard to connect with your child without first understanding where they are. As counselors and speakers at parenting events across the country, we spend a great deal of time teaching parents about development. To know where your child is—not just physically, but emotionally, socially, and spiritually, helps you to truly know and understand who your child is. And that understanding is the key to connecting.

The *Phase Guides* give you the tools to do just that. Through the research of the Phase Project, *Phase Guides* are an insightful, hopeful, practical, and literal year-by-year guide that will help you to understand and connect with your child at every age.

Jennifer Walker, RN BSN

Author and co-founder of Moms On Call, mother of three

These resources for parents are fantastically empowering, absolute in their simplicity, and completely doable in every way. The hard work that has gone into the Phase Project will echo through the next generation of children in powerful ways.

Tina Naidoo

Executive Director of The Potter's House of Dallas, Inc

It's true that parenting is one of life's greatest joys but it is not without its challenges. If we're honest, parenting can sometimes feel like trying to choreograph a dance to an ever-changing beat. It can be clumsy and riddled with well-meaning missteps. If parenting is a dance, this *Phase Guide* is a skilled instructor refining your technique and helping you move gracefully to a steady beat.

For those of us who love to plan ahead, this guide will help you anticipate what's to come so you can be poised and ready to embrace the moments you want to enjoy.

Carlos Whittaker

Speaker, storyteller, best-selling author of multiple books, including *How to Human*, father of three

Not only are the *Phase Guides* the most creative and well-thought-out guides to parenting I have ever encountered, these books are essential to my daily parenting.

With three kids of my own, I know what it's like to swim in the wake of daily drama and delicacy. These books are a reminder to enjoy every second. Because it's just a phase.

Cheryl Jackson

Founder of Minnie's Food Pantry, award-winning philanthropist, grandmother

As the founder of Minnie's Food Pantry, I see thousands of people each month with children who will benefit from the advice, guidance, and nuggets of information on how to celebrate and understand the phases of their child's life.

Too often we feel like we're losing our mind when sweet little Johnny starts to change his behavior into a person we do not know. I can't wait to start implementing the principles of these books with my clients to remind them... it's just a phase.

David Thomas, LMSW

Co-director of Family Counseling, Daystar Counseling Ministries, speaker, and author of 10 Books including *Wild Things: The Art of Nurturing Boys*, father of three

I began exploring this resource with my counselor hat on, thinking how valuable this will be for the many parents I spend time with in my office. I ended up taking my counselor hat off and putting on my parent hat. Then I kept thinking about friends who are teachers, coaches, youth pastors, and children's ministers, who would want this in their hands.

What a valuable resource the Orange team has given us to better understand and care for the kids and adolescents we love. I look forward to sharing it broadly.

Josh Shipp

Best-selling author of *The Grown-Up's Guide to Teenage Humans*, award-winning speaker, teen expert, father of three

As I speak to high school students and their parents, I always wonder to myself: What would it have been like if they had better seen what was coming next? What if they had a guide that would tell them what to expect and how to be ready? What if they could anticipate what is predictable about the high school years before they actually hit?

These *Phase Guides* give a parent that kind of preparation so they can have a plan when they need it most.

Danielle Strickland

Speaker, global social activist, author of *The Other Side of Hope*, mother of three

The *Phase Guides* are incredibly creative, well researched, and filled with inspirational actions for everyday life. Each age-specific guide is catalytic for equipping parents to lead and love their kids as they grow up.

I'm blown away and deeply encouraged by the content and by its creators. I highly recommend Phase resources for all parents, teachers, and influencers of children. This is the stuff that challenges us and changes our world. Get them. Read them. And use them!

Courtney DeFeo

Author of *Treasured* and *In This House* and *We Will Giggle*, podcaster, mother of two

I have always wished someone would hand me a manual for parenting. Well, the *Phase Guides* are more than what I wished for. They guide, inspire, and challenge me as a parent— while giving me incredible insight into my children at each age and phase. Our family will be using these every year!

PARENT CUE

Parenting Your New Baby

A GUIDE TO MAKING THE MOST OF
THE "I NEED YOU NOW" PHASE

THE PHASE PROJECT

Parenting Your New Baby:
A Guide to Making the Most of the
"I Need You Now" Phase

Published by Orange, a division of The reThink Group, Inc.,
5870 Charlotte Lane, Suite 300, Cumming, GA 30040 U.S.A.

Parent Cue ® is a registered trademark of The reThink Group, Inc.
It's Just a Phase ® is a registered trademark of The Phase Project, LLC.

ISBN: 978-1-63570-213-2
© 2024 The Phase Project, LLC

Printed in United States of America
Second Edition 2024
1 2 3 4 5 6 7 8 9 10
06/01/2024

Special thanks to —

JON ACUFF for guidance and
consultation on having conversations about
technological responsibility

JIM BURNS, PH.D for guidance
and consultation on having
conversations about sexual integrity

JEAN SUMNER, MD for guidance
and consultation on having
conversations about healthy habits

CHINWÉ WILLIAMS, PH.D for guidance and
consultation on how to navigate crisis

Every educator, counselor,
community leader, and researcher
who invested in the Phase Project

In Partnership →

Parent Cue partners with the Phase Project, designing Phase Guides to help you parent your child through every year in the four main phases: Preschool, Elementary School, Middle School, and High School.

The Phase Project →

Started in 2013, the Phase Project is a synthesis of personal experience, academic research, and gatherings of leaders and educational experts from across the child development spectrum.

Contents

How to Use This Guide

The guide you hold in your hand doesn't have very many words, but it does have a lot of ideas.

Some of these ideas come from thousands of hours of research. Others come from parents, educators, and volunteers who spend every day with kids the same age as yours. This guide won't tell you everything about your kid, but it will tell you a few things about kids at this age.

The best way to use this guide is to take what these pages tell you about babies and combine it with what you know is true about your baby.

After each idea in this guide, there are pages with a few questions designed to prompt you to think about your kid, your family, and yourself as a parent. The only guarantee we give to parents who use this guide is this: You will mess up some things as a parent this year. Actually, that's a guarantee to every parent, regardless. But you, you picked up this book!

You want to be a better parent. And that's what we hope this guide will do: help you parent your baby just a little better, simply because you paused to consider a few ideas that can help you make the most of this phase.

Let's sum it up:

Things about babies

+

Thoughts about your baby

=

Your guide to the next 52 weeks of parenting

Dear Parent,

Welcome to a new phase!

REGARDLESS OF HOW MANY FRIENDS, FAMILY MEMBERS, and perfect strangers try to paint an accurate picture of parenthood, there's nothing anyone can say that adequately prepares you for that heart-stretching moment you hold your newborn for the very first time.

And the sentiments only grow exponentially from there. There aren't words in any language capable of conveying the myriad of emotions you will experience as a new parent. Love. Gratitude. Exhaustion. Fear. Joy. Frustration. Excitement. Hate.

(Okay, you won't really hate your baby. Just the sound of your baby crying at three in the morning when it's only been half an hour since her last feeding.)

Maybe that's the best word to describe the new baby phase: emotional. It's emotional for you. It's emotional for them. But despite the crying—both yours and theirs—there is something indescribably wonderful about that first year of life.

Somewhere along the way, in the delirium of teething and feedings and diapers and sleep schedules, something almost magical takes place. It's in the way your baby smells after a bath, wrapped in a towel and lying on your chest. It's in the way their eyelids flutter when they sleep. It's in the shape of their perfect little mouths, the length of their tiny fingernails, and the velvety feel of their skin against yours. There's something alluring about the way that they are totally and completely brand new.

In my work as a preschool director, my favorite rooms to visit were the ones assigned to this age group. These were my volunteers' favorite rooms, too. People literally wait in line to hold a baby. To rock a baby. To ooooh and ahhhh over baby's impossibly long eyelashes or new hair bow.

There is a great sense of promise that adds to the allure of this age. Literally, anything is possible. The pages of their story are gleamingly blank, striking with potential.

As a parent, you have many phases ahead, and each one has its own set of unique possibilities. But right here, right now, you have something you will never have again—at least not in this way. You could think about it like this: You will never have messed up less as a parent than you have at this moment. Really. This is the beginning. You have a fresh start. And even though it's scary, even though you don't know what you're doing (none of us do), you have everything you need—you.

That's right. Because, despite the thousands of mass-marketed baby products available, there is only one thing your baby really needs right now—your baby needs you.

Some days it may seem like they need you a little too much, or a little too often, or a little too immediately. Don't worry. With every passing month, they will discover a new ability that lets them need you a little less. But for now, in this fleeting new baby phase, they need you. And you are enough.

Sweet joy and pride so big it hurts—this is what wells up in the hearts of moms and dads as they watch their new baby develop into a little person with opinions and intellect and personality. And as you gaze, you begin to realize what this really means. Not only do you get a ringside seat to watch the beauty of potential form right before your eyes, but you get the joy of helping influence, train, and build who your child will become.

Just remember: There will come a day when your once-helpless baby will bathe, dress, and feed himself, but the journey to get there comes with a little mess along the way.

Holly Crawshaw

Preschool director, educator, author, mother of three

52 Weeks to Parent Your New Baby

WHEN YOU SEE HOW MUCH TIME YOU HAVE LEFT, YOU TEND TO DO MORE WITH THE TIME YOU HAVE NOW.

For some, this phase sounds like...

● words you may say

What's that smell?

No one told me that.

It's your turn.

WHY. ARE. YOU. CRYING?

We are out of diapers.

I'm just going to drive around the neighborhood for another hour.

Should I nap, or should I shower?

I can't stop crying.

That's the most beautiful face I've ever seen.

Shhh, Shhh, Shhh, Shhh

Did I eat today?

Should we call the doctor?

There are approximately **936 weeks** from the time a baby is born until they grow up and move to whatever is next.

Right now, that might seem like <u>a lot of weeks.</u> The future probably still feels far away and full of possibility. But the truth is your baby will grow up faster than you ever dreamed.

That's why every week counts. Of course, each week might not feel significant. There may be weeks in your baby's first year when all you really accomplish is feeding them. That's okay.

Take a deep breath. You don't have to get everything done this week.

But what happens in your child's life week after week, year after year, adds up over time. So, it might be a good idea to put a number to your weeks.

Measure It Out

HINT:

If you want a little help counting it out, you can download the free Parent Cue app on all mobile platforms.

JOURNAL

How many weeks do you have with your child until they graduate and move to whatever is next?

Write down the number.

Create a Visual Countdown

Find a jar and fill it with one marble for each week you have remaining with your child. Then make a habit of removing one marble every week as a reminder to make the most of your time.

Where can you place your visual countdown so you will see it frequently?

Which day of the week is best for you to remove a marble?

Is there anything you want to do each week as you remove a marble?

HINT:
*Say a prayer,
write in a baby
book, retell
one favorite
memory from
this past week.*

*Bonus idea—
place the
marble you
removed into
a second jar
so you can see
how much time
you've invested
in your child.*

You only have <u>52 weeks</u> with your new baby while they are still a baby.

Then they will be a toddler, and you will never know them as a baby again. That might be incredibly emotional, or it might be the best news you've heard all day.

Or to say it another way:

> **Before you know it, your baby will grow up a little more and...**
> → **sleep through the night.**
> → **play independently.**
> → **learn to tell you what's wrong.**

Just remember, the phase you are in now has remarkable potential. Before their first birthday, there are some distinctive opportunities you don't want to miss.

So, as you count down the next 52 weeks, pay attention to what makes these weeks different from the rest of the weeks you will have with your child as they grow.

EVERY PHASE IS A TIMEFRAME IN A KID OR TEENAGER'S LIFE WHEN YOU CAN LEVERAGE DISTINCTIVE OPPORTUNITIES TO INFLUENCE THEIR FUTURE.

Reflect

What are some things you have noticed about your baby in this phase that you really enjoy?

What is something new you are learning as a parent during this phase?

The phase when nobody sleeps, everything smells, and one mesmerizing baby convinces you, "I need you now."

You've never known sleep deprivation like this.

Maybe that's why every book on babies seems to be primarily dedicated to keeping them happy (stop the crying, please!) or helping them sleep longer (so you can sleep longer).

You've never really smelled like this.

When faced with the choice between sleep or a shower, there are days (no one's counting how many) when cleanliness doesn't win out. The smells aren't all bad though. Just watch how long it takes grandma to lean over and sniff a new baby the first time they meet.

You've never been needed like this.

Your baby needs you more desperately, more consistently, and more frequently than at any other stage of life. They need you to feed them, clean up their messes, and help them get to sleep. They need you to comfort them, smile at them, and entertain them. And although the days can be long and the tasks can feel demanding, only one thing matters most at this phase—you show up.

Every new baby is unique.

Even with unique babies—which yours most certainly is—most babies have a few things in common. This book will show you what those are so you can make the most of the "I Need You Now" phase with your baby.

Remember: We haven't met <u>your</u> baby. This book is just about a lot of babies.

Some may sleep through the night at six weeks old.

Some don't sleep through the night for another six years.

Some may cry when you put them in their car seat.

Some cry unless you put them in their car seat.

Some start walking by the time they are seven months old.

Some start thinking about trying to roll over by that time.

Some will poop once a day.

Some will poop ten times a day.

Some will look just like Aunt Kiki.

Some will look like no one you have ever seen before.

Some may swim the length of a 25-meter pool by nine months.

(Yours probably won't.)

Some want to suck on a pacifier, some want to suck on their thumb.

Some want to suck on everything.

This year, your new baby is changing.

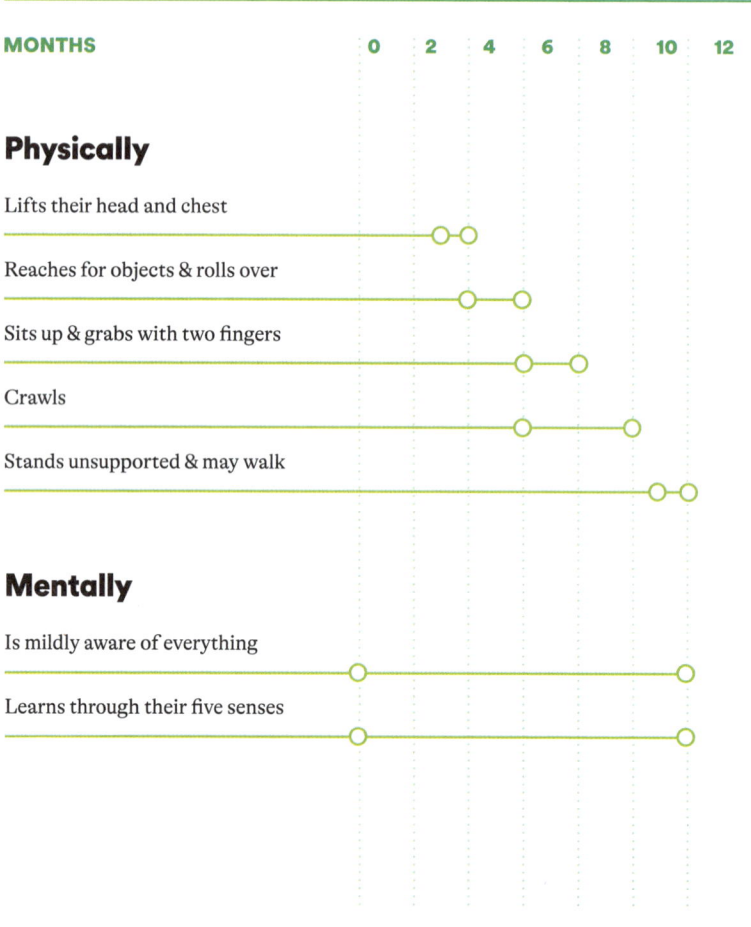

MONTHS   0   2   4   6   8   10   12

Physically

Lifts their head and chest

Reaches for objects & rolls over

Sits up & grabs with two fingers

Crawls

Stands unsupported & may walk

Mentally

Is mildly aware of everything

Learns through their five senses

| MONTHS | 0 | 2 | 4 | 6 | 8 | 10 | 12 |

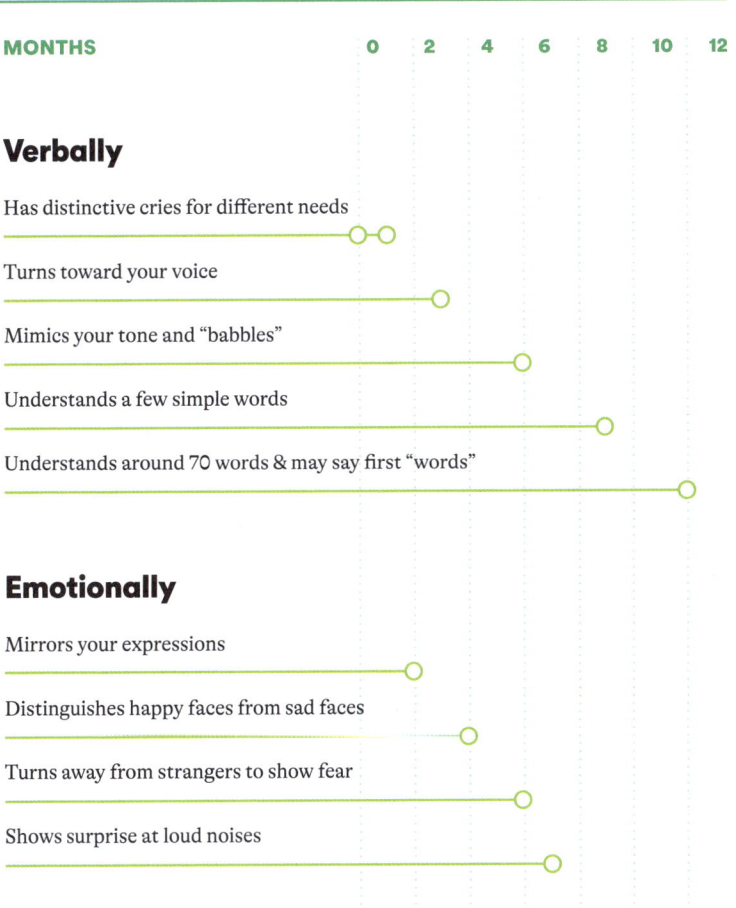

Verbally

Has distinctive cries for different needs

Turns toward your voice

Mimics your tone and "babbles"

Understands a few simple words

Understands around 70 words & may say first "words"

Emotionally

Mirrors your expressions

Distinguishes happy faces from sad faces

Turns away from strangers to show fear

Shows surprise at loud noises

What are some changes you are noticing in your baby?

You may disagree with some of the characteristics we've shared about babies. That's because every baby is unique.

What makes your baby different from babies in general?

What do you want to remember about your baby's first year?

HINT:
There are enough lines for at least one per week. Throughout the year, write down a few simple things you want to remember.

First Holidays

Your child will have only one first Christmas, one first Valentine's Day, and one first birthday. That can seem like a lot of pressure to get it right. Here are some thoughts to consider as you celebrate a year of firsts:

Relax: Your baby's first holidays are more about you than them. Your baby won't remember the decorations, if you invited their best friend, or if they got any presents. So...

Do what fits your style:

→ If you like to throw big parties and host many guests, go for it.
→ If you prefer small celebrations with just family, enjoy keeping it simple.
→ If you get stressed out by spending "unnecessarily," don't.

Create new traditions: The traditions you create now will create memories for a lifetime. Try a few this year and see what sticks. You can build on them over time.

Reflect

Who are the essential people in your life you want to celebrate your baby's firsts with?

What are some celebration traditions you remember fondly or have seen other people do that you liked?

Six Things Every Kid Needs

WHEN YOU SEE HOW MUCH TIME YOU HAVE LEFT, YOU TEND TO MAKE WHAT MATTERS, MATTER MORE.

It's worth repeating: When you see how much time you have left, you tend to make what matters, matter more.

Depending on your personality, that can sound empowering, or just like a lot of pressure. Relax. Every day doesn't have to create a memory worth posting.

The important thing to remember is a countdown clock doesn't mean you try to squeeze more things into each week so you can get the most out of it. It actually means acknowledging that you can't do what you can't do.

You can't make your child always behave in public. But over time you can show them the kind of love that is the foundation for how we treat each other.

You can't make your child make wise choices. But over time you can introduce them to stories that widen their perspective and inform their decision-making.

You can't make your child be a good friend. But you can give them safe places to belong so they will know that people matter.

You can't make your child perform at the top of their class. But you can make learning fun, and use mistakes as opportunities to grow.

This week matters because it's an opportunity to give your baby a few things that really matter. You can't do what you can't do. Let some things go, and you might just discover you're already doing more significant things than you ever realized.

Your kid needs six things over time.

Over the next 936 weeks, your child will need many things.

Some of the things your kid needs will change from phase to phase, but there are six things that every kid needs at every phase. In fact, these things may be the most important things you give your kid—other than food. Kids need food.

The next few pages are designed to help you think about how you will give your baby these six things, right now—before they turn one.

Every kid, at every phase, needs:

 **Love** to give them a sense of *worth*.

 **Stories** to give them a bigger *perspective*.

 **Work** to give them *purpose*.

 **Fun** to give them *connection*.

 **People** to give them *belonging*.

 **Words** to give them *direction*.

No. 1

Every kid needs **love** over time to give them a sense of **worth.**

One question your baby is asking:

Your baby has suddenly arrived in a world where... no one speaks their language. They are unsure how to coordinate their movements. They have limited control over their next meal, next bath, or next nap. Your baby is asking one major question: **"Am I safe?"**

As the parent of a baby who may cry more than you imagined, or sleep less than you had hoped, or poop more than you thought possible, your role may feel overwhelming at times. But remember this—in order to give your baby the love they need in this phase, you need to do one thing: **Embrace their physical needs.**

The way you show up hour after hour, day after day, to feed, change, and soothe your baby is establishing a foundation of trust that will follow them for the rest of their life.

Reflect

You are probably doing more than you realize to show your baby just how much you love them.

HINT:

You may need to look at this list on a bad day to remember what a great parent you are.

Write down the schedule for a typical day that you might spend with your baby. Make a list of what you do for your baby and how much time it takes.

JOURNAL

Showing love requires paying attention to what someone likes.

What does your baby seem to enjoy the most right now?

It's impossible to love anyone with the relentless effort
a baby demands unless you have a little time for yourself.

*What can you do to refuel each week so you are able to give your baby the
love they need?*

Who do you have around you supporting you this year?

No. 2

Every kid needs **stories** over time to give them a bigger **perspective.**

Books to read to your baby:

Giraffes Can't Dance:
Touch and Feel
by Giles Andreae

Whose Toes Are Those?
by Jabari Asim

B is for Baby
by Atinuke

Dear Zoo:
A Lift-the-Flap Book
by Rod Campbell

The Very Hungry
Caterpillar
by Eric Carle

Who Takes Care of You
by Hannah Eliot

We All Play
by Julie Flett

Time for Bed
by Mem Fox

Toot Toot Beep Beep
by Emma Garcia

Think Big, Little One
by Vashti Harrison

Black on White
by Tana Hoban

Sleepyheads
by Sandra J. Howatt

Where Is Baby's
Belly Button?
by Karen Katz

Brown Bear, Brown Bear,
What Do You See?
by Bill Martin Jr.

First 100 Words
by Roger Priddy

Numbers Colors Shapes
by Roger Priddy

Baby Cakes
by Karma Wilson

Goodnight Moon
by Margaret Wise Brown

HINT:
*You can find a
more in-depth
reading list at
ParentCue.org.*

55

Reflect

Kids need the kind of stories you will read to them over time. But they also need family stories.

What can you do this year to capture your family's story so you can retell the story of this year to your child when they are older?

What makes your family history unique? How can you preserve the story of your family's history for your child?

Are there other stories that matter to you? What are they, and how will you make them a part of the first 52 weeks of your baby's life?

No. 3

Every kid needs **work** over time to give them **purpose.**

Work your baby can do:

→

Follow moving objects with their eyes
(2-4 months)

Hold their head up
(tummy time, 3-4 months)

Reach, grasp, and hold on
(4-6 months)

Roll over
(4-6 months)

Sit up
(6-8 month)

Crawl
(6-10 months)

Pull up on furniture
(9-10 months)

Clap their hands
(8-10 months)

Stand up
(11-12 months)

Point
(9-12 months)

Take a first step
(12-15 months)

61

Reflect

What are some things your baby has worked to accomplish so far?

How are you holding back to give your baby the space they need in order to do things on their own? And how do you reward their efforts?

What are things you hope your baby will be able to do independently in the next phase?

How are you helping your baby develop those skills now?

No. 4

Every kid needs **fun** over time to give them **connection.**

Ways to have fun with your baby:

Toys

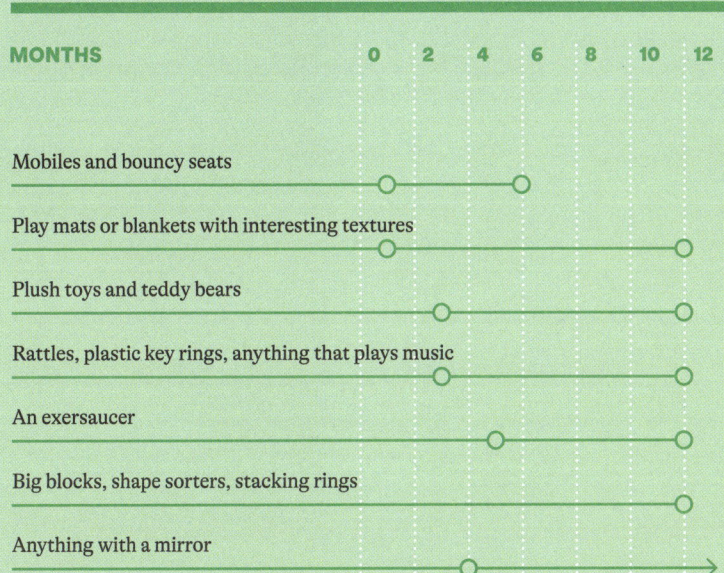

MONTHS	0	2	4	6	8	10	12

Mobiles and bouncy seats

Play mats or blankets with interesting textures

Plush toys and teddy bears

Rattles, plastic key rings, anything that plays music

An exersaucer

Big blocks, shape sorters, stacking rings

Anything with a mirror

Activities

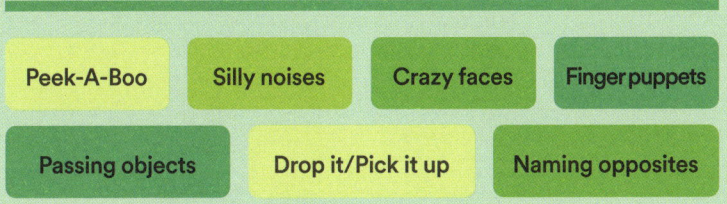

Peek-A-Boo

Silly noises

Crazy faces

Finger puppets

Passing objects

Drop it/Pick it up

Naming opposites

Reflect

What are some activities that make you and your baby laugh?

When are the best times of the day, or week, for you to set aside to have fun with your baby?

This year, your baby will have some important celebrations.

What are some ways you want to have fun on these special days?

First Birthday

Holidays

No. 5

Every kid needs **people** over time to give them **belonging.**

Adults who might influence your baby:

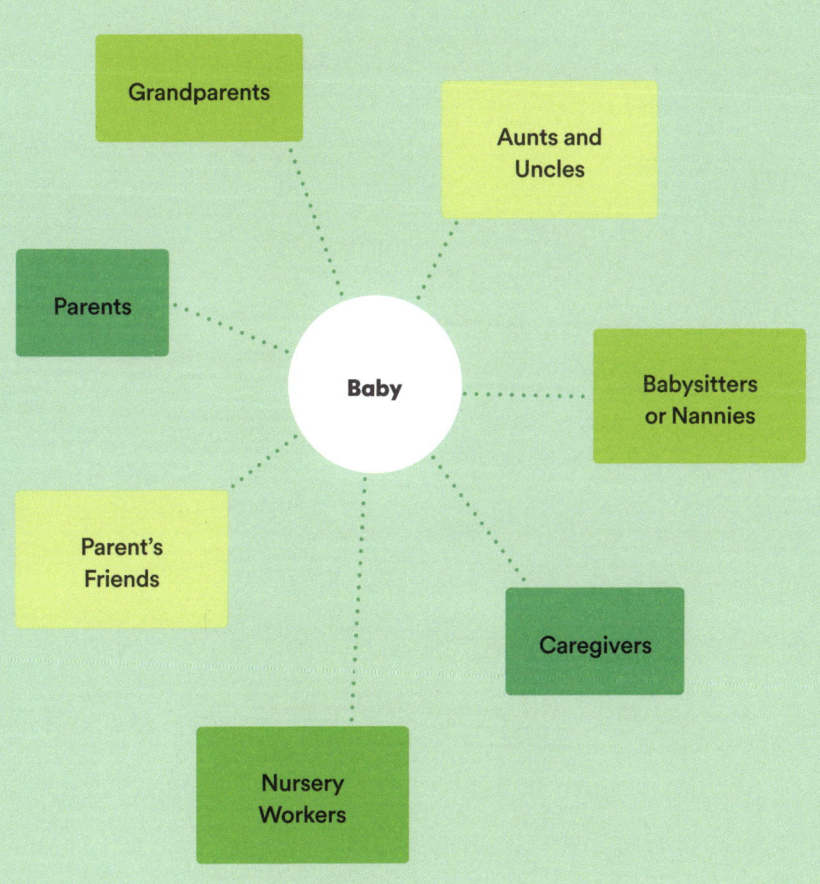

- Grandparents
- Aunts and Uncles
- Parents
- Baby
- Babysitters or Nannies
- Parent's Friends
- Caregivers
- Nursery Workers

Reflect

HINT:
They're probably the adults your baby reaches for and doesn't shy away from.

List at least five adults who have influence in your baby's life right now.

What is one way these adults could help you and your baby this year?

EXAMPLES:
*Pray for you,
bring a meal,
maybe even
hold the baby
while you get
some sleep.*

What are a few ways you could show these adults appreciation for the significant role they play in your baby's life?

No. 6

Every kid needs **words** over time to give them **direction.**

Words your baby needs to hear:

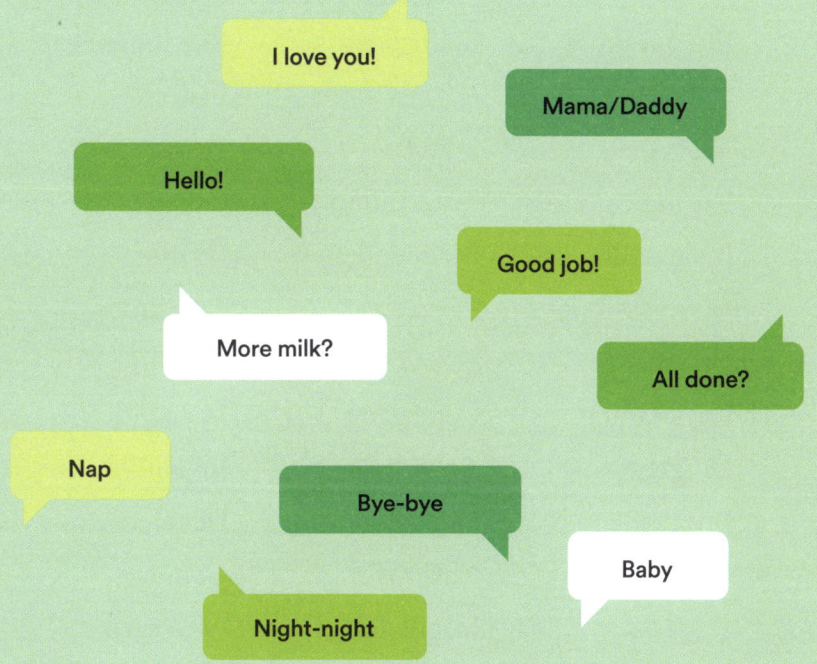

Improving your child's vocabulary will help them in the phases to come. Here are a few ways you can help:

① Talk to your baby—the more, the better.
② Speak slowly and clearly.
③ Make eye contact.
④ Point at objects when you name them.
⑤ Repeat the same word a lot.

Reflect

What word (or words) describe your hopes for your baby in this phase?

Determined	Motivated	Gentle
Encouraging	Introspective	Passionate
Self-Assured	Enthusiastic	Patient
Assertive	Joyful	Forgiving
Daring	Entertaining	Creative
Insightful	Independent	Witty
Compassionate	Observant	Ambitious
Amiable	Sensitive	Helpful
Easy-Going	Endearing	Authentic
Diligent	Adventurous	Inventive
Proactive	Honest	Devoted
Optimistic	Curious	Genuine
Fearless	Dependable	Attentive
Affectionate	Generous	Harmonious
Courageous	Committed	Empathetic
Cautious	Responsible	Courageous
Devoted	Trustworthy	Flexible
Inquisitive	Thoughtful	Careful
Patient	Loyal	Nurturing
Open-Minded	Kind	Reliable

Where can you place those words in your home so they will remind you what you want for your baby this year?

Babies understand approximately 70 words by their first birthday.

What are some of the first words you hope your baby hears and understands?

WHEN YOU see HOW MUCH TIME YOU HAVE LeFT, YOU TeND TO VALUe WHAT HAPPeNS OVeR TIMe.

The most important things we give our kids aren't the gifts we just give once, but the ones we give over time. Just remember...

 We don't experience worth because we are loved once, but because we are **loved** by someone over time.

 We don't understand the world through a single event, but through a collection of **stories** over time.

 We don't usually discover our purpose in one great revelation, but through consistent opportunities to **work** over time.

 We don't develop trusted relationships in a day, but we become connected to others through laughter, **fun**, and shared experiences over time.

 We don't know we belong because of a single invitation, but because we have been welcomed by **people** over time.

 We are not motivated to action by one statement, but by **words** that move us over time.

Four Conversations to Have in this Phase

WHEN YOU KNOW WHERE YOU WANT TO GO, AND YOU KNOW WHERE YOU ARE NOW, YOU CAN ALWAYS DO SOMETHING TO MOVE IN A BETTER DIRECTION.

Over the next 936 weeks of your child's life, some conversations may matter more than others.

What you say, for example, regarding **pirates, spiders, and football** might have less impact on their future than what you say regarding **health, sex, technology, or faith.**

The next pages are about the conversations that matter most. On the left page is a destination—what you might want to be true in your kid's life 936 weeks from now. On the right page is a goal for conversations with your baby and a few suggestions about what you might want to say.

Healthy Habits

Learning to strengthen my body through exercise, nutrition, and self-advocacy

This year you will establish basic nutrition so your child will have consistent care and experience a variety of food.

You may not have conversations with your baby regarding healthy habits in this phase, but you will talk with someone about your child's health.

Say things like...

Hey Mom, do you know our family medical history?

Ask grandparents and relatives for a health history.

How do you know if he's getting enough to eat?

Decide where you will go to get good advice about your baby's health.

When should we schedule our next appointments?

Prioritize well visits with your pediatrician at 1, 2, 4, 6, 9, and 12 months

Reflect

HINT:

Okay, "exercise" may be a stretch, but tummy-time counts.

What are your goals for providing your baby with good nutrition and exercise?

Who will help you monitor and improve your baby's health?

What are your own health goals for this year? How can you improve the habits in your own life—even in a phase when your most common health question might be, "Should I use their nap time to sleep or shower or eat?"

Sexual Integrity

Guarding my potential for intimacy through appropriate boundaries and mutual respect

This year you will <u>introduce them to their body</u> so your child will discover their body and define privacy.

Your conversations with your child regarding sexual integrity will never be simpler than they are right now. But it's never too early to start with some of the right words.

Say things like...

God made your strong little legs.

God made your elbows.

God made your vagina/penis.

Use correct names of body parts as you bathe and change your child—experts suggest that learning proper words can protect your kid from potential harm as well as create a positive view of their body.

Reflect

HINT:

*Parents,
media, friends,
other adults...*

What influences shaped your views of sex growing up?

How does your own life story shape your future hopes for your child in this area?

When it comes to your child's sexuality, what do you hope is true for them 936 weeks from now?

Are you and your spouse, or your child's other parent, on the same page when it comes to talking about sex with your child?

How might you work on a plan to communicate your hopes and expectations about sex through real-time conversations with your child?

Technological Responsibility

Leveraging the potential of online experiences to enhance my offline community and success

This year you will enjoy the advantages so your child will experience boundaries and have positive exposure.

In spite of research that warns you to absolutely never allow your baby to make eye contact with a screen, technology has some incredible benefits for you and your baby. Practically speaking, it's not too soon to begin asking yourself a few questions about technology.

Say things like...

Does it really matter if I forgot to record the last feeding in the app?

Answer: No. As long as the baby ate, she does not care.

Is there anyone out there who can relate?

Use technology to connect to other adults.

Look at this baby!

Take as many photos as you like. You will enjoy seeing them later.

Reflect

What kind of digital access was available to you when you were growing up?
How have things changed since then?

What are some issues you think may come up as you raise your child in a digitally connected world? Where can you go to find advice to help navigate those issues?

When it comes to your child's engagement with technology, what do you hope is true for them 936 weeks from now?

What are your own personal values and disciplines when it comes to leveraging technology? Are there ways you want to improve your own savvy, skill, or responsibility in this area?

Authentic Faith

Trusting Jesus in a way
that transforms how I love
God, myself, and the rest
of the world

This year you will incite wonder so your child
will know God's love and meet God's family.

Your baby isn't ready to make a public
declaration about what they believe, but that
doesn't mean you can't begin to lay a foundation
for their faith. In this phase, incorporate faith
into a few of your daily routines.

Say things like...

God, thank You for this healthy baby.

Pray aloud while you are with your baby.

Jesus loves me.

Sing songs while you hold your baby.

We are going to church!

Connect with a faith community.

Reflect

Who will help you develop your child's faith as they grow?

Is there a volunteer at your church who shows up consistently each week for your child? Do you attend a consistent service so your baby can begin to feel familiar with the leader who greets them?

When it comes to your child's faith, what do you hope is true for them 936 weeks from now?

What routines or habits do you have in your own life that are stretching your faith?

Rhythms and Responses

The rhythm of your week will shape the values in your home.

Now that you have filled this book with dreams, ideas, and goals, it may seem as if you will never have time to get it all done. Actually, you have 936 weeks. And every week has potential.

The secret to making the most of this phase with your baby is to take advantage of the time you already have. Create a rhythm to your weeks by leveraging these four times together.

Morning Time

Set the mood for the day. Smile. Greet them with words of love.

Feeding Time

Reconnect throughout the day. Make eye contact and hold them close.

Cuddle Time

Be personal. Spend one-on-one time that communicates love and affection.

Bath Time

Wind down together. Provide comfort as the day draws to a close.

Reflect

What seem to be your baby's best times of the day?

What are some of your favorite routines with your baby?

Write down any other thoughts or questions you have about parenting your baby.

Preparing for the Unexpected

Parenting humans at any phase of life is filled with the unexpected.

No matter the age, sometimes the unexpected discoveries we make as parents may elicit fear, anger, or confusion as we try to guide our kid toward a positive future. It may even be something that is completely out of our control, like a medical diagnosis or a family tragedy. That's why it's best to create a response plan when you are clear and thoughtful.

So, take a few, deep breaths. Find a place where you feel safe and comfortable. If you need to walk away and come back to this at a later time, that's okay, too.

Download → parentcue.org/preparing

Reflect

Every parent has what it takes to navigate challenges with their kids, but none of us can carry the weight alone.

HINT:

Think of someone with whom you feel safe enough to be completely honest about what is happening and what you are feeling.

JOURNAL

If you were to discover something you weren't expecting in your kid's life, who would you be able to call?

_____

_____

_____

_____

_____

_____

How would you begin that conversation?

_____

_____

_____

_____

_____

_____

_____

_____

_____

Every kid who is navigating challenging situations needs their parent's involvement. But a parent may not be the only influence they need.

If you were to discover something you weren't expecting, who else in your kid's life could you count on to walk with them through this experience?

_____

_____

_____

_____

_____

_____

What might you want to go ahead and share with them about your kid and/ or your family?

_____

_____

_____

_____

_____

_____

_____

_____

_____

Navigating
Crisis

What is a crisis?

Even though you are a great parent, you won't be able to protect your baby from everything. You may have already figured this out by now, but you aren't in complete control—at least not all the time. There may be times when your baby will experience a crisis. A crisis for your baby can be any physical or emotional threat.

How do you recognize it?

Because your baby can't tell you what's going on, recognizing they may be experiencing a crisis can be especially difficult. Watch for these three things:

① Are they regressing?

Regressions are a primary indicator of a crisis. Your baby may suddenly begin waking up during the night, become more clingy, or experience separation anxiety.

② How are they expressing themselves?

Your little one may be more cranky or irritable than usual, be clingy, refuse food, or stop gaining weight.

③ How are they sleeping?

Growth spurts, teething, or reaching new milestones can sometimes cause sleep regression, which usually lasts 2-4 weeks. If it lasts longer, there may be something else going on.

How do you respond to it?

Responding consistently with warmth and gentleness helps your baby feel safe and builds a secure attachment. This connection buffers the effects of any crisis they may be experiencing, whether big or small.

① Re-establish some routine.

Routine provides comfort and a sense of safety. Keep their feeding, play, and sleep times predictable. But also follow your baby's cues and body language to understand when your baby needs more sleep, food, or an extra dose of cuddle time with you.

② Connect.

Increase your "connection" time by being physically close. Cuddle, snuggle, rock, and dance with your baby. Sing favorite and familiar lullabies, and offer gentle and comforting words. Try swaddling them in a large, thin blanket to provide an extra sense of security.

③ Play music.

Listening to music is a great calming technique for you and your baby, whether you are rocking your baby in your arms or swaying to the rhythm of the beat. Play slow, soft, repetitive music to slow down your baby's heartbeat and initiate a sense of calm.

④ Take care of yourself.

Babies can absorb their parents' stress. Prioritize your own self-care by getting rest when you can, exercising, and eating well. Call a friend or family member for emotional support. Accept help when offered, and get professional help if needed.

When do you need outside help?

You can expect parenting to come with many challenges. But when the challenges are persistent despite your best efforts, don't try to go it alone. Reach out to a pediatrician or an expert in infant and early childhood development.

What's Next: The One-Year-Old Phase

In only 52 weeks you will rediscover your baby as a one-year-old.

One of the joys of parenting is the many surprises that greet you around every corner.

We can't prepare you for all the joys that await you in the next phase, but we can give you a glimpse of a few things that might help you anticipate what's coming.

The one-year-old phase may look like...

Helping them climb the stairs

Sippy cups and straws

Saying "no" on repeat

Rolling the ball back and forth

Kissing boo boos when they lose their balance.

Chasing them around the house

Letting them push all the buttons

Watching them scribble on everything

Hearing them learn to use words

In not so many weeks you may discover an emerging one-year-old who is ready to show you, **"I can do it."**

One-Year-Old

The phase when nobody's on time, everything's a mess, and one eager toddler will insist, *"I can do it."*

Expect to be late.

Maybe you had to wait for your toddler to "do it myself" (just try and stop them). Or maybe they impressively filled a clean diaper just as you got into the car. Whatever the reason, this phase will make even the most punctual adult miss the mark occasionally.

Look forward to a few fashion statements.

Expect a few mismatched outfits, magic marker tattoos, sticker collages, and other various states of creative expression. In this phase, you will choose not only your battles, but also which messes will just have to be tolerated.

Their struggle for independence has begun.

You feel it the first time they try to feed themselves and dump applesauce down the front of their shirt. Just remember, by letting them do some things "myself," they're not only learning new skills, they're also developing the confidence they need in order to move to the next phase.

The Phase Timeline

HINT:

The full Phase Timeline is available at parentcue.org/ timeline.

About the Timeline

The one thing that is true across every phase is that your child will change—and so will your role as a parent. The phase timeline is a visual to help you see the progression through their first 18 years. Reference it over time to remember where you have been and to get an idea of where you are heading.

About the Curve

Your child will also experience different levels of intensity across the phases. Watch for where the line rises to know when your child may be experiencing more developmental intensity. Whenever that seems overwhelming, this timeline is a reminder that it's just a phase.

Remember: We haven't met your kid. This timeline is just what's true for a lot of kids.

Preschool → Your role is to embrace their physical needs.

Elementary School → Your role is to engage their interests.

Middle School → Your role is to affirm their personal journey.

High School → Your role is to mobilize their potential.

The Preschool Phase

Your Role →

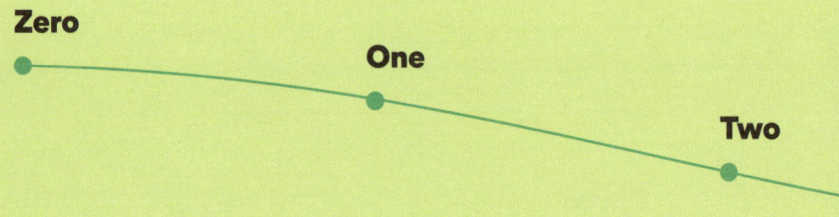

Embrace their physical needs.

Zero

One

Two

New Baby	**One-Year-Old & Two-Year-Old**
Wants to know...	**Wants to know...**
Am I safe?	Am I able?
So...	**So...**
Establish trust.	Develop their confidence.

Thinks Like →

A preschooler thinks like an artist, so engage with their senses.

Motivated By →

A preschooler is motivated by safety, so respond consistently.

Three

Four

Three-Year-Old & Four-Year-Old

Wants to know...

Am I okay?

So...

Cultivate their self-control.

It's just a phase, so don't miss it.

Be the parent you want to be with Parent Cue.

We believe in every parent's ability to be the parent their child needs. Good parenting takes on many forms!

Parent Cue is here to cue you with what you need, when you need it—curated content, weekly inspiration, free resources, products, and more—so you are equipped to be the parent you want to be.

Get started → parentcue.org

Parent smarter, not harder.

Make the most of everyday moments on the go. Download the free Parent Cue app to get weekly cues and content to connect with your kid in every phase from New Baby to Twelfth Grade—available for iOS and Android. Weekly phase content also available with an in-app subscription.

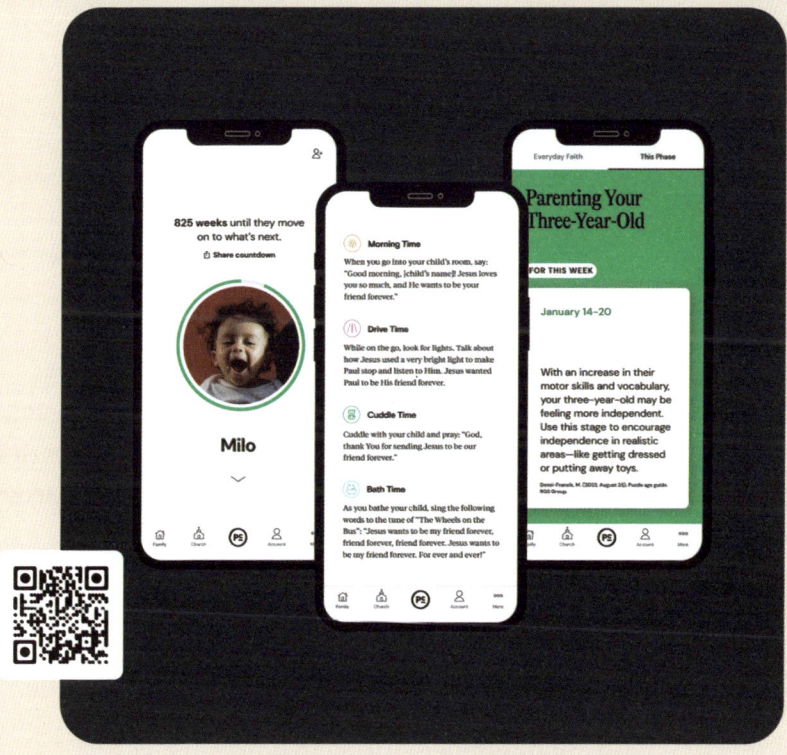

Download now → parentcue.org/app

Ready for the next phase.

These guides are the core product of the Phase Project—a synthesis of personal experience, academic research, and gatherings of leaders and educational experts from across the child development spectrum.

Just like this one, each guide will help you make the most of every phase in your child's life through:

① What is changing about your kid
② The six things your kid needs most
③ Four conversations to have each year
④ Rhythms and responses
⑤ What's next

A guide for every phase.

This guide is one of an eighteen-part series, so you can follow your parenting journey across every phase from New Baby to Twelfth Grade.

Preschool Phase	Elementary School Phase	Middle School Phase	High School Phase
New Baby The "I need you now" Phase	**Kindergartner** The "Look at me!" Phase	**Sixth Grader** The "Who Cares" Phase	**Ninth Grader** The "This is Me Now" Phase
One-Year-Old The "I can do it" Phase	**First Grader** The "Look at me!" Phase	**Seventh Grader** The "Who's Going?" Phase	**Tenth Grader** The "Why not?" Phase
Two-Year-Old The "I can do it" Phase	**Second Grader** The "Sounds like fun!" Phase	**Eighth Grader** The "Yeah... I Know" Phase	**Eleventh Grader** The "Just Trust Me" Phase
Three-Year-Old The "Why?" Phase	**Third Grader** The "Sounds like fun!" Phase		**Twelfth Grader** The "What's Next?" Phase
Four-Year-Old The "Why?" Phase	**Fourth Grader** The "I've Got This" Phase		
	Fifth Grader The "I've Got This" Phase		

Shop now → phaseguides.com